PRINCIPAL
DUSANEK

BY THE STUDENTS OF
WASHINGTON ELEMENTARY SCHOOL

1st WORLD
PUBLISHING

Principal Dusanek

by the students of Washington Elementary School

© 1st World Library - Literary Society, 2005
1100 North 4th St. Suite 131, Fairfield, Iowa 52556
• Tel: 641-209-5000 • Fax: 641-209-3001
• Web: www.1stworldlibrary.org

First Edition

LCCN: 2006900687

ISBN: 1-595-40981-5

Editing and Cover Design: Anya Charles & Aman Charles

Mr. Dusanek

We will all miss you a lot. I hope you will have fun
training dogs. Oh yeah, thanks for the gummy
worms you gave me for the treats for birthdays. I
hope you liked my treats.

Roses are red, violets are blue,
I know your retiring, and I will miss you.

Roses are red, violets are blue,
you are my friend, and I will miss you.

by your friend: Allison Petersburg

Dear Mr. Dusanek

Roses are red, violets are blue,
I am so sad, that I will miss you.

Why do you have to retire? You are my favorite
principal. Well, you are the only principal I've had
so far. If you think you are getting old you have to
be crazy because you do not look old at all.

by your friend: Ashley Ann Evard

To Mr. Dusanek

Mr.Dusanek,it is sad that
you are retiring, but thanks
for all you've done.

The End

by Colton Putnam, 4th grade

Mr. Dusanek

Mr. Dusanek you're a great guy, I really don't want
to say good bye.
You're tall and nice and, do you like rice?
Your ties are really fun, I like them a ton.
But anyway, I just wanted to say, you're really cool
in every way!

by Erin Thompson

To: Mr. Dusanek

Yo, Mr. Dusanek, we're gonna miss you here. So
why do you have to leave, cause we like you here?
So, please don't leave. Come on, stay.

by Isaac Capetillo

Mr.Dusanek

Rose's are red, violets are blue, school is cool, and so
are you.
We'll miss you!

by Jenna Nelson

Mr.Dusanek it is true that you will leave.
But no matter what you know it is true,
I will never forget you.
See ya later,

by Jenna Nelson, 4H

To: Mr. Dusanek

Mr. Dusanek you've been here for about ten years.
What's your favorite animal? I like dogs and wolves.
Did you ever know Mr. Dooley?
Are you going to raise dogs when you retire?
Will you see your grandchildren all day long?
Or, will you sit back and remember the good old
days as a principal?

by Josh Dimmitt

We'll miss you Mr. Dusanek.
Mr. Dusanek Awesome, Cool

Laughing, helpful, in charge, our principle, good,
school's owner, friend, best person in the world,
full of hope.

by Joshua Alonso

Mr. Dusanek

Mr.Dusanek you make me smile you make me
smile. You make me smile for a little while. Okay.
Okay. You got my attention. If I don't smile
I'll get detention.

by Katrina Jackson

Mr. Dusanek

Mr. Dusanek let's see.... Ummm... oh yes, he's funny, caring, nice, thoughtful, and respects other peoples opinions. He's been a principal for like.. ever! But he's been a great principal. When he retires will he take vacations? Will he build a dream house? Well.. I sure don't know, but he's been a great principal!

by Kayla Septer

To: Mr. Dusanek

Why do you have to retire? What if a strict, mean principal comes? Why can't you stay? I like the rules you put down. I like how you do things. So I'll see you later? I might see you at the grocery store, maybe. Please stay here!

by Kyle Hunte

Mr. Dusanek

Thanks for being my principal and helping me with a lot of things. Like my first year at school. Why do you want to retire? And good luck. Mr.Dusanek,

by Luis Giron

We'll miss you dear.
I wish you could stay another year.
I'm mad that you're leaving. I will be very sad.
I wish I Knew where you're going.
I guess where the wind is blowing.
I hope you don't go to Maine because
that can be a pain.
I hope you will visit. I hope I won't miss it.

by Mason Carnahan

Stupid Smelly Bus

Who invented the bus?
Not that I'm having a fuss
I just don't like the bus.
It has a stench
Worse than a splinter in a bench.
I just don't like the bus!

by Michaela Burgmeier

Mr. Duasanek

We are really going to miss you. I hope you don't go
far. I would really like to see you after you retire.
We are really going to miss you. Thank you for all
your help. We will miss you.

by Randy Andermann

Gummy Worms

Gummy Worms, Gummy Worms, Slimy, gooey,
ushy, mushy Red and Yellow, Green and White
All they come in my delight
And when I think I think of him I always think of
Gummy Worms.

by Sidney Baumann, 2005 4H

Mr. Dusanek

Mr. Dusanek
he is a great guy,
he laughs, he plays,
he's a great principal,
Mr. Dusanek!

by Tori L. Keltner

Mr. Dusanek

Mr. Dusanek you were the best principal I ever had.
I will remember when you joke around with me
and my sister. You were nice and funny.
You're pretty tall too.
I'll always remember you.

by Tyler Cooksey

To: Mr. Dusanek

You are the nicest principal I have ever had.
You don't make me mad.
You're really cool, at the best school.
You rock the town, and all around.
You should not retire, because I'm not a liar.
You rock, and I would never ever mock.

by Wyatt Andersen

Mr. Dusanek

He has white hair and nice as a dog,
He ran the school today.
I don't want him to go,
I wish he would have a good life.

by Hunter McLain

Mr. Dusanek

nice and funny,
you run the school with grate care,
as rough as stone,
I wish you have the best of your years.

by Madison Nelson

Mr. Dusanek

Kind and friendly,
Helps out the school,
As gentle as a butterfly,
I wish he would stay here.

by Laura Jackson

Mr. Dusanek

nice and funny
he is a principal and does it well
he's as funny as Jim Carey
I wish he wouldn't retire

by Alex Shier

Mr. Dusanek

you are funny but tough,
Our principal is happy because we're nice,
as tough as a guard dog,
I wish you could stay.

by Dorian Jean Larson

25

Mr. Dusanek

nice and kind,
funny as a clown,
Our perfect principal,
I wish you visit us at
Washington Elementary School.

by Emily Giovannetti

Mr. Dusanek

Cool and nice,
He's the man of the school,
As nice as a dog,
I wish wasn't retiring.

by Jacob Heiisel

Mr. Dusanek

nice and funny,
Our school principal likes us
because we're nice to him,
As strong as a tough man,
I wish he didn't have to retire.

by Jake McLain

Mr. Dusanek

amazing and nice.
He is the principal.
He makes sure we are happy.
He is as nice as a grandparent.
I wish he would stay my principal for ever.

by Lalita Martin

Mr. Dusanek

nice and funny,
nice principal,
As funny as a clown
I wish you have a grate retirement.

by Paige Palmer

Mr. Dusanek

serious but funny,
The person in charge of everything.,
As funny as a monkey,
I wish you could stay our principal.

by Riley Hammel

Mr. Dusanek

Nice and friendly ,
Our principal takes care of all of us,
As nice as a teddy bear,
I wish Mr. Dusanek a happy life.

by Sashmere Wright

Mr. Dusanek

Super nice and funny,
He is the best principal there could be. I don't
now how he does it, but he does,
As happy as a hippo,
I wish you didn't have to go Mr. DUSANEK.

by Eden Marie Bell

Mr. Dusanek

Nice and funny
He takes good care of us by being a good principal,
As nice as a bunny,
I wish Mr. Dusanek wasn't retiring

by Erin Enright

Mr. Dusanek

nice and funny,
The guy who is in charge of the school,
as funny as a monkey,
I wish YOU DIDN'T HAVE TO RETIRE.

by Halie Nicole Fankhauser

Mr. Dusanek

Funny but Tough
The guy that runs the school.,
As nice as a puppy
I wish You wouldn't leave.

by Jaclyn Grace Flinspach

Mr. Dusanek

cool and rocks.
he's in charge of the school he takes care of stuff.
he's the best principal ever.
I wish he wouldn't retire.

by Jonah Dowell

Mr. Dusanek

Hard working and buff,
The person that is in charge of the school.
As nice as a puppy
I wish you wouldn't retire.

by Keith Burns

Mr. Dusanek

Funny and nice,
As funny as a loon,
I wish Mr.Dusanek will have a good retirement
and a happy life.

by Landon Thomas Gamrath

39

Mr. Dusanek

Nice and cool,
The man who owns this school,
s funny as a joker,
I wish he could stay longer

by Matthew Juarez

Mr. Dusanek

funny and playful,
He is our principal,
as busy as a bee,
I wish you didn't have to retire!

by Taalia Larson

Mr. Dusanek

Good principal at Washiington.
Mr D
Really friendly! you aren't
Don't forget us.
You are a nice principal. You are nice

by Lilliana Montgomery

Children is who he likes.
Outside giving us new equipment.
Our person we love.
Love you!!
Sounds like he's retiring.
Cool person.
He was here every day I was
Out of the ordinary.
Out of our room.
Like us.

by Meghan Shelangoski

Mr. Dusanek

Merciful to others
Rambunctious

Different than other principals
Unusual
So Cool
Awesome
Nicer than other principals
Exciting
King of the school!!

by Nick Jackson

Mr. Dusanek

Careful - leaving might be a mistake!
Real careful
You - no you're not mean
Intelligent and really nice
No, don't leave us please!
Golly - did you say "Retire!"

by Reilly Harbison

Mr. Dusanek

Proud
really sweet
incredible
nice
cool
intelligent
people like him
awesome
leaving us

by Tracy Andermann

Mr. Dusanek

Such a good principal
Cool
Happy
Our favorite person
Oh, don't leave
Leaving? Why are you? ...are with drawings. ...are
with drawings.

by Trent Taglauer

Retirement
Excellent
Terrific
Incredible
Read
Excitement
Miss us
Eat
Ninety years old
The best man

by First Grade Authors

Trae Van Tasell, Jarrett Hellweg
Drew Stever, Tylor Rooney, Dain Nelson,
Melissa Callan

Master
Read
Desk
Useful
School
A sleep
Nice
Earth
Kind

by First Grade Authors

Trevor Drish, Zack Price, Alex Landon-
Hahn, Michael Hodges-Sisco, Nathan
Thompson, Paige Holderbaum, Taylor
Ferrell

Washington
Awesome
Smart Kids
Small Hands
Impressive
Names
Great
Teachers
Out of here
Naughty Kids

by First Grade Authors

Emma Kuehl, Giovanni Cingire, Katie
O'Brien, Sydney Rowe, Christine Spears,
Alexis Magram

Mr. Dusanek

Mr. Dusanek you are great.
You gave me the gummy worms that I ate.

Mr. Dusanek you taught me very much.
At this school I get my lunch.

Mr.Dusanek I learned a lot of things.
'Till I heard the bus bell ring.

When it was my birthday, I started to squirm.
Because I wanted some jelly worms.

Well, here is something I can't believe.
That you will have to retire and leave.

by Adam Gevock

Mr. Dusanek

My principal is very nice
Really great

Delightful
U are funny
Shares yummy gummy worms
Always keeps us safe
Nice
Excellent principal
Kind to everyone

Mr. Dusanek, we will really miss you next year!

by Ms. Adam's Kindergarten Class
2004-2005

Mr. Dusanek

Kind to kids
I'm wondering where are you going to work?
Now we will miss you
Dear Mr. Dusanek - please don't leave.

by Bryce Lunsford

Mr. D

You're the best principal ever!
I wish that you wouldn't retire from
Washington School because.......
You're funny
and
You like to tease children!!

by Dalton McCarroll

Mr. Dusanek

Good, good, good person
Oh, don't forget me
Oh, don't forget anybody
Don't retire please!!

by Douglas McDowell

Mr. Dusanek

You are a cool principal.
You are a great principal.
We won't be able to find
another principal as great as you!!

by Dyllan Light

Mr. Dusanek

Mr. Dusanek
Really nice

Don't forget us
yoU are great
Stay
Astounding
Nice to everyone
Extremely funny
Kind to kids

by Evan Wood

Mr. Dusanek

Funky and funny and cool
Unique dude
Neat and sharp as a tack
Kind and radical
Your rock Mr. Dusanek - please don't leave!

by Gareth West (not Will)

School

Sad
Cool.............Not
How could you leave us?
Oh I'll miss you,
On your way, don't go.
Leaving? why?

you are nice!!!!!!!!!!!!!!!!!!!!!!!!!!!!!!!!!!!

by Hannah Agan (not trouble)

Retires

Recommendations none.
Entertaining, too. Stay!
Terminating disappointment.
I beg you. Don't go!
Recking our unhappiness!
Eh? How's that? You are?!
Seriously, Don't move!

by Ian Gottshall

Mr. D

When Mr. D leaves the school I will feel sad!
I will miss his funny jokes!!
Please, Please Stay
Mr. Dusanek!!

by Jolea Burkhart

Mr. Dusanek

Mr. Dusanek is
Rare. He calls me
Double Trouble. He likes
Us
So much!
A
Nice guy like you isn't
Enough for
Karley!!

by Karley Williams

Mr. Dusanek

I will miss you VERY much.
I think you're funny,
You cheer me up!
Happy retirement!

by Kotie Webber

Mr. Dusanek

I really care about you, I really do! Please don't retire. I want to thank you, you are a great principal. Wherever you're going, I hope you are not going too far. I don't want you to go for, because I want to see you at a store.

HAPPY RETIREMENT!

by Ashrita Singh

Mr. Dusanek

We know you are retiring,
But we like your funny jokes.
We never wanted you to leave this school!
We hope you come back.
We are sad, we are crying,

DON'T LEAVE PLEASE!!!

by Austin Hagans

Mr. Dusanek

Mr. Dusanek,
I am sad,
I'll miss you really bad,
When you leave.

by Baylie Dimmitt

Mr. Dusanek

We will miss you,
And we wish you would stay.
I really don't want you to go away.
You make us laugh sometimes.
I think you're the best principal ever!

by Crystal Grimm

Mr. Dusanek

Magic
Real cool

Don't retire
Uses funny jokes
Super
As cool as can be
Nice
Every day he makes us smile
Kidding us

by Dillan Carlson

Mr. Dusanek

Mr. Dusanek,
You are really funny
you're as cute as a bunny
(I was just joking about that)
But you do have a funny hat!!
And... you are the best principal in the world!!!

by Fransesca Greco

Mr. Dusanek

Mr. Dusanek, I will miss you.
Really, I will miss you, Mr. Dusanek.

Dear Mr. Dusanek, I am unhappy.
Us, a nice good-bye to the school.
Sad when you are gone.
As a kind and nice principal, please stay.
Nice principal, Mr. Dusanek.
Every principal should be nice like you.
Kind and gentle principal, you are.

by Gannon Haile

Mr. Dusanek

I really appreciate everything you do for this school.
I am sad you are retiring .
You are the coolest principal!

Your friend, Gretchen Greiner

Mr. Dusanek

Mighty nice
Real Happy

Did a great job
Understanding
So good
A good principal
Nice and happy
Everybody will miss you!
Kind to everybody

by Logan Fleeman

Mr. Dusanek

Mr. Dusanek, you are so cool,
Mr. Dusanek, please stay at our school!
Mr. Dusanek, please don't retire,
Mr. Dusanek, you're leaving too soon!

by MacKenzie McLure

Mr. Dusanek

Mr. Dusanek, I like you a lot
I will miss you
But, I hope you will visit us,
You are a great principal
I hope you'll have fun
Being retired!!

by Madison Roberts

Mr. Dusanek

Magic
Real funny

Don't retire
Ultra cool
Strong
As funny as a clown
Nice
Every day he makes us laugh
Kind

by Narenda Martain

75

Mr. Dusanek

I will miss you when you are gone.
You are a very nice principal with shining eyes.
Why are you retiring?
What will you do after you are gone?

by Parm Banwait

Mr. Dusanek

Mr. Dusanek, I think you are a good principal.
I am sad, I am mad that you are leaving.
I wish you could stay,
don't go away.
Thank yo for being my principal.

HAPPY RETIREMENT!

by Phineas

Mr. Dusanek

Oh, Mr. Dusanek, we wish you could stay.
Will you come back and visit us some day?

by Robbie Kloski

Mr. Dusanek

Mighty nice
Real happy

Daily jokes
Usually giving us different names
Sad you are leaving
After you retire I hope you visit us
Nice and funny
Everybody's favorite principal
Kidding us

by Shey Worth

Mr. Dusanek

Mr. Dusanek, we like you so much.
We're sorry you're leaving,
it's hard to say Good-bye!!!
Please stay, we like you here.
It's not fun without you,
we like how you are funny
and how your make us laugh!!

HAPPY RETIREMENT!!!!!!!!!!!!!!

by Sidney Adam

Mr. Dusanek

I will miss your jokes and I will
miss how your eyes sparkle

I will mis you a lot Mr. Dusanek,
And I will miss you making me laugh.

I will miss you saying, "stop smiling."
And i will miss you saying
"Get that smile off your face, Whitney."

You know i will miss you when you leave!!!!!!!

by Whitney Guyette

Mr. Dusanek

Mr.Dusanek I have to say your the best principal
I've ever had
Other principals sometimes made me mad
Your nice and kind and generous
And your fun and humorous
Even though you can't remember my name
Your a great guy

by Arianna Hickey

M is for many jokes you tell
R is for retiring after so many years

D is for dedicated principal
U is for being you
S is for you smiles
A is for all the activities you do
N is for always being nice
E is for an excellent principal
K is for the kindness you show

GOOD BYE

by Cierra Bielinski

Good-Bye
Good-Bye Mr. Dusanek
I'll miss you and
the way you call me
one of my sisters.

Good-Bye Mr.Dusanek
I'll miss when you
ask whose Birthday is
it and when you get out
my splinters.

Good-bye Mr. Dusanek
I'm gonna miss your
funny tricks and jokes.
Good-Bye

by Claire Slechta

Dusanek

You are funny sonny
You were a great funny principal.
You were a great person to solve promblems too.
You were nice and funny to other kids.
Thanks for the gummy worms you gave us.
You were nice at this school.

by Holly Kerr

Mr. Dusanek

Mr nice
Rock on.end of career

Dusanek
U rule
Super
A principal
Not Knotty
Every day is good
Knot perfect

by Jacob Adam

Mr.Dusanek, thank you for five great years at
Washington School.
Every moment was spectacular!
You were caring and fun.
We will all miss you greatly
I wish you could stay. You made school what it is
supposed to be.
Thank You!

by Jacquelyn Bell

Mr. Dusanek

More than great!
Rock on!

Da bomb!
U rock!
Smiling every day!
A good principal!
Nice work!
Everybody likes ya!
Kind & trustful

by Jonathan A. #2

Mr. Dusanek

Mr.Dusanek thanks for three great years at
Washington. You were the BEST! You always made
me smile. You taught us all to care for one another.
I know we all will miss you very much. I wish you
could stay one more year.
Katie Anderson
In your words as Betty B-bop

by Katie Anderson

M is for Mr.
R is for red gummy worms.

D is for Dusanek.
U is for usually nice.
S is for super nice.
A is for apples.
N is for NO never tell you no.
E is for eating sweets.
K is for kind.

by Lacey 17

My favorite person
Really cool

Doesn't give detentions.
Upper league
Super nice
Awesome
Nice
Especially nice
Knows everything

by Mason12

Mr.Dusanek

I hope you had a great time at Washington School.
And I will miss you and all the kids in Washington
School. Will miss you to And I hope you have a
nice retirement.

by Matt14

Makes school fun
Really nice and advisive

Does a good job as a principal
U were a good principal
Sixty-four is the age you retire
Always helpful
Never mean to others
Everyone will miss you
Kind in every way

by Ricky Guernsey

Made school fun for everyone
Really pleasant

Did good things for the school
U?I can' t think of anything that starts with U
Some really long word that I can' t spell
Always pure.PS.Use the thesaurus

by Spencer

Mr. Dusanek

Mr. D.
friendly, tall,
helping, caring, laughs,
leader, loves funny jokes,
plays, helps, loving,
smiles, cares,
principal.
Good-bye Mr. Dusanek!

by Alexs Van Dijk

Mr. Dusanek

Mr. Dusanek we appreciate you.
For all the things you do.
Your safety patrol.
Is in control.
You won't take a dog to the pound.
Because you'll miss that hound.
Your retirement comes to mind.
Because you are so kind.
We'll miss you, Mr. Dusanek.

by Miranda Williams, Allison Hoffman,
and Sandra Avila

Mr. D

Mr.D is so cool
'cause he was principal of this school
He's the best around
'cause he rarely has a frown
Mr.D is gonna retire
We will miss him
Bye, Mr.D.

by Chelsea and Sammy

How We Do

This is how we do; we leave the school on the last day.
This is how we do; me and D are acting a fool.
Fresh like ahhh! Pencil grip ahh.
D and came and got Max from the spot.
Sprinting out the school. Last day.
This is how we do; we leave the school on the last day.
This is how we do; me and D are acting a fool.
Gave D the keys, so he could be first.'
In on switch room, that desk so low D got all the
janitors playing that fool.
Cody, ahhh! D, ahhh!
I'm the one who wrote this song.
Took two months, but I got it done.
Mr.D signed out of Washington and made some money.
D-D-D-D-Unit!

by Cody Kool

How He Does

Fresh like uh Ds #1
It's his last year here
But he got it done
It's his last year here
D no more, that really stinks
thats what everyone thinks
D-D-D-D-D-D unit

by Cobrin Harwood

Mr. Dusanek

I know this poem's not really great,
But you'll have to accept it because it's all I've got.
This poem, as said before, I know you'll hate.
But at least you'll be happy to know, I gave some thought.
I thought about what I'd say,
and what it would mean to you,
I then decided on this one,
Out of all the teachers that have taught,
You have hit really high on my chart,
and a lie, that is not.

Let joy fill your life forever more,

by Darien Maxwell Sloat

Mr. D

Mr. D
funny, caring
building, helping, trying
school, Fairfield, principal, kids
smiling, listening, playing
neat, nice
Mr. D

by Haley W, Marcella D, Monica S

Mr. Dusanek

Mr. Dusanek
Has good taste in ties
Mr. Dusanek
has been here long
Mr. Dusanek
has to say "so-long"
Mr. Dusanek
Were glad you stayed so long

by Jessica

Du-ta-Du Song

Du-ta-Du-ta-Du Duseanek is the man.
Du-ta-Du-ta-Du Duseanek has a plan.
Du-ta-Du-ta-Du Duseanek is the one.
Du-ta-Du-ta-Du Duseanek can get it done.
Du-ta-Du-ta-Du Duseanek is the principal.
Du-ta-Du-ta-Du Duseanek is going to be missed
by the school.

D-D-D-D-D UNIT!

by Max Johnson and Davis Lowenberg

Mr. Dusanek

Mr. D, your nice, because you give us a fun time at school, and not a bad time at school. You never put anybody down before, and that's what I like most about you. You never made me frown.

by Megan Palmer

Mr. Dusanek

I've enjoyed you coming to our school because you
made it fun.
I've enjoyed you coming because you're nice to
people. I've enjoyed you coming because you help
people with their work.
I've enjoyed you coming to our school because you
always put a smile on my face.
I've enjoyed you coming because you keep every-
thing organized (including Mrs. Miller).
I've had a great time with you, K-5 grades.
I hope you will always remember the school just
like I will next year in middle school.
I hope you remember all the students that you've
met (including me).
If you always remember me,
I will always remember you.
I hope you have a happy/great retirement.

by Michael Gooki

Mr. Dusanek

Mr. D you're so cool,
Too bad that you are leaving school.
Have fun training dogs,
We'll be writing in our learning logs.
HAPPY RETIRMENT!!!!!!
See you later,
Alligator.

by Shannan Baker

Mr. Dusanek

You are going to retire,
So we wish you a happy retirement.
And we want to know, where are you going to live?
Maybe you will go to Hong Kong,
Or Santa Fe, New York, or even Broadway.
But then again you will go home.
But we do not know why you are leaving, because
you look like your in your mid 30s.
When we're eating lunch,
you make us a jolly good bunch.
What we are trying to say is we are going to miss
you. 1 One out of ten, you're a 100,000!

HAPPY RETIREMENT, MR. DUSANEK!!!

by Storm Hultine & William West

Mr. Dusanek

Mr. Dusanek, I just want to say
that I look forward to each day
even though your not here Saturday and Sunday
These have been the greatest years
and I think everyone should hear
that your the best principal here

by Abby McMahon

Mr. Dusanek

Mr. Dusanek, Mr. Dusanek
You're so funny, You're so funny
I wish you could stay with me,
So I could see you every day.

by Alec Stoner

For Mr. Dusanek

We all know you've had
A great last year!
But for us kids,
It gives us fear.
We don't know who'll be here,
We don't know who they'll send,
And we hope and pray
We will make to the end.
WE WILL MISS YOU!

by Alex Gookin

The D Man

You have been here for a long time. When I first
came to school, I was scared, you were nice, and
you were cool. You play with kids, how sweet. You
listened to our Ensemble songs. Now, how can any-
one beat that?

Your sky blue eyes so clear and happy, I feel sorry
for the children who will not have you. Mr.
Dusanek you've been awesome, and you've been
great. We'll miss you!

You've been an amazing principal. One thing I want
you to do, is try out for president,
please and thank you.

by Anya Charles

Mr. Dusanek

We will always remember you, the way you ran this school. We will miss you forever and ever. The way you said to me "Don't say never."

by Braz Johnson

Mr. Dusanek

Mr.D Mr.D you're so fine, you're so fine you blow my mind. You're so mine, if you want someone else that is fine, but you're still real fine.

The End

by Brent Buch

Mr. Dusanek

Mr. Dusanek,

Who could ask for a better principal? A question more likely asked. Who would want to ask for a better principal? Well, anyway Mr. Dusanek, Larry, which ever one you prefer, I hope you have a really spectacular retirement. I wish you (and your dogs) a very, very happy life.
Maybe your favorite student,
Haven Tichey

P. S. This message might self-destruct in five seconds.
I guess it didn't. Well, I hope you have a happy retirement.

by Haven Tichey

Please don't retire

Roses are red
Violets are blue
Please don't retire
Because we'll miss you- Jessica Enright

by Jessica Enright

Dude is so
unspeakably
special
as
nice as
everyone is
kool

by Jessica Enright

We Will Miss You

Roses are red, violets are blue, Mr.D you're great,
we will miss you!

by Kaylen Marlay

Mr Dusanek

If youre sad about leaving then I'll sing you a song.
Dont worry, be happy oooohoooohoohooyeye-
woooweoooweooo don't worry, be happy now.
My message was to make your day better and don't
worry be happy here's another one
hey MR.D you're so cool you're so cool you make
girls drool, oh yea, uh huh I said you're so cool you
make kids rule.

YEA SAY WHAT

PS. IM SO SAD ILL MISS YOU EVERYONE
WILL
HOPE TO SEE YOU OUT OF SCHOOL SOME
TIME.

by Logan Hoffman

Mr Dusanek

Mr.Dusanek you're so fun,
Mr.Dusanek you're #1.
Mr. Dusanek you're so cool,
Mr.Dusanek I'll miss you and school.
Mrs. Dusanek you've been fun since grade 1,
Mr. Dusanek you've got perfect touch,
and 'll miss you so very much.

by Angela Michelle Spears

Mr Dusanek

Listen my classmates,
and you shall hear,
of a principal who is going to retire this year.
In the beginning of school in 2005,
a new principal is going to arrive.
The new principal will not be as nice and as funny,
because no one is like Mr. Dusanek.
I know this poem is pretty stupid,
but I did my best so get used to it.

by Mukund Martin

Mr Dusanek

roses are red
violets are blue
we will miss you
very much
Mr. Dusanek

by Nicole Burke

Mr Dusanek

Mr.D is so cool
I wish he wouldn't retire
He made me drool
So much I laughed
He's a very fun principal
He liked little kids, and me too
I know you had to work in an office
and you had to be in there a lot
We know you liked working at Washington School
And everybody will miss you

by Nikki S.

#1 Principal

Mr.D u are #1,
u are the best, because your just the best.

by Q-Tip (Quinton B.)

An Acrostic Poem for Mr. Dusanek

Mature
Reliable

Dominate of our school
Understanding
Smart
Nice
Emancipating from our school
Kind

Mr. Dusanek this is a brief description of you. You
are a great principal. We'll miss you.

by Sarah Flinspach

Why Retire?

Why retire when the school needs you,
Why retire when you need them too.
Why retire when you've been here so long.
Why retire when all you've done is good
Why don't you retire when we say you should,
We're going to miss you,
We hope you miss us too,
Please come back do not leave,
You made people believe,
That they could smile every time they see you,
You made me believe too,
So let me ask you this one question,
Can I tell you this suggestion,
Why retire?

by Serena W.

Wishing You Were Here

We're wishing you were here till the sun goes up,
We're wishing you were here to save another pup.
We hope you'll miss us,
because we miss you.
We never wanted you to go,
but thanks for everything.
We're wishing you were here till we moved out of own,
because of you Mr. Dusanek, you.
We'll miss you,
Mr. D

by Shannon Cochran

Mr. Duesanek

Great
Best Friend
Don't go yet
Great Principal Nice

by Skyler Bartholomew

Stay

Why so long,
why now?
Stay, you are young,
you are nice.
Stay nice some more you lucky principal.

by Trevor Williams

Good Bye Mr. Dusanek

You've been our principal for all the years
You've been so kind to us for all the years
You've settled problems for all the years
You've helped us for all the years
You've been a friend for all the years
You've dealt with us for all the years
You've made us learn for all the years
We will miss you for all the years

by Tyler Breeding

Our Principal

We will always remember Mr. Dusanek, our principal,
because he is

Funny   Cameron
Nice   Paige
Great   Aman
Always happy   Mikaela
Smart   Ryan
A great principal   Holly

We will always remember Mr. Dusanek, our
principal, because he

Likes kids   Halie
Likes being a principal   Olivia
Likes teachers   Madison
Likes children   Alex
Gives us "gummy" worms   Brandon H.
Writes a lot   Tyler
Likes us   Kailey
Likes what kids make   Navin
Likes dogs   Matthew
Smiles   Sukh
Lets us be first graders   Manasi
Wears Mickey Mouse ties   Mitchell
Wears cool shirts   Lane

Mr. Dusanek, our principal, is retiring

I like him   Brandon S.
I will miss him   Addison

by Mrs. Moore's Kindergarten Class
2004-2005

Mr. Dusanek, Our Principal

Mr. Dusanek, you rock
Radical

Decent
Ultimate
So cool
Awesome
Nice
Excellent
Kind

by Christopher Callen

Mr. Dusanek, Our Principal

Makes us better people
Radical

Dogs you train
U (you) love dogs
Super nice
A help
Nice guy
Eagles you like
Kind

by Gage Cook

Mr. Dusanek, Our Principal

Marvelous mega fun
Radiant

Dogs, you love them!
Understands us
Songs he loves them
A nice terrific person
Nice and lovable
Excellent principal
Kind and respectful

by Aspen Light

Mr. Dusanek, Our Principal

Mickey Mouse is cool like you!
Really nice

Dogs you really like
Understands
St. Louis Cardinals, you don't like!
Are a good principal
Never lies
Extra special
Kind

by Kara Greiner

Mr. Dusanek, Our Principal

Mega fun
Really nice

Dude
U (you) rock
St. Louis Cardinals - Boo!
A good person
Nice teacher
Excellent
Kind

by Austin Greenfield

Mr. Dusanek, Our Principal

Pal
Raises yellow and black Labradors
I think you are kind and fun.
Nice
Considerate
I think you are nice.
Pal
A good guy
Loyal

by Dalton Price

Mr. Dusanek, Our Principal

Many people like you
Really nice to kids

Decent principal
Unforgetful
St. Louis - Ugh!
Awesome at everything
Nice to everyone
Excellent at training dogs
Kansas rocks too!

by Matthew Carr

Mr. Dusanek, Our Principal

Promising
Radiant
I will miss you!
Nice
Courteous
Intelligent
Pal
A really nice Guy
Lots of fun!

by Vincent Horras

Mr. Dusanek, Our Principal

Mega Fun!
Really nice

Dependable
U (you) rock
Smart
A good person
Nice
Excellent
Kind

by Austin Greenfield

Mr. Dusanek, Our Principal

Magnificent
Rocks

Dogs
Understandable
ST. Louis Cardinals - Boo!
A perfect principal
Nice
Expert person
King of the school

by Coren Hucke

Mr. Dusanek, Our Principal

Promising
Raises Labradors
I will miss you
Nice
Cares
I like you
Penguins I like
A nice guy
Lots of fun

by Mason Ellis

Mr. Dusanek, Our Principal

Memories
Radiant

Doesn't lie
Understands
Super Cool
Always loves us
Nice
Everybody love you
Kind

by Summer Heckethorn

Mr. Dusanek, Our Principal

Mega Cool
Raises Labradors

Dogs
Understands
Shining
A fun guy
Nice
Exciting
Kind

by Valerie Payne

Mr. Dusanek, Our Principal

Miss You!
Really nice

Doesn't lie
Ultra nice
Super cool
Always loves us
Never lies
Everybody loves you
Kind

by Charan Williams

Mr. Dusanek, Our Principal

Perfect, never change
Really Cool
Incredible
Nice team
Cardinals - Blah!
I think you are funny
Pal
A super nice guy
Loves children

by Allison Angstead

Mr. Dusanek, Our Principal

Miss you
Raises yellow and black Labs

Decent
Understands
Special
Always there when you need him
Nice
Excellent
Kind

by Rachel Biggs

Mr. Dusanek, Our Principal

Mr. Mega fun
Radiant

Dude
USA proud
Superific
A perfect guy
Nice
Excellent
Kind

by Claudia Sloat

Mr. Dusanek, Our Principal

Mickey Mouse ties
Raises and trains Labradors

Doesn't like Cardinals
Understanding
School
A nice person
Neck ties
Excellent
Kind

by Aubreann Loving

Mr. Dusanek, Our Principal

Principal
Raises and trains Labradors
I have a dog named Harley
Nobody can take you place
Cares about us
I like your pen
Pals around with us
A great principal
Looks after us

by Dani Cassiday

Mr. Dusanek, Our Principal

Marvelous
Raises Labradors

Does like helping
Understands us
Special
A perfect role model
Nice and friendly
Excellent
Kind to teachers

by Baylee Bowman

151

Mr. Dusanek, Our Principal

Mr. Nice Guy
Raises dogs

Dogs love you too!
U (you) are nice
So Incredible
A nice guy
Nice
Excellent
Kind

by Keri Schwarz

Mr. Dusanek, Our Principal

Miss you
Raises a lot of dogs

Do good
Useful person
Saves a lot of dogs too
A very good person
Nice guy
Eat good
Kind person

by Nick Rich

Mr. Dusanek, Our Principal

Mr. Dusanek rules the school
Ruler

Dogs are cool and you know it!
Ultimate fun!!
Super Cool!!!
A very cool principal you are
Now you are retired
Extra cool, and awesome
King of the school

by Adian Hodges

Mr. Dusanek, Our Principal

Mega Man
Rolls smoothly

Dodgers rule
Ultra cool
St. D. rules
Amazing
Nobody is better
Extra nice
King of principals!

by Max Spalla

Mr. Dusanek, Our Principal

Marvelous
Remarkable

Dazzling
Unique
Sharp
Amazing
Nice
Excellent
Kind

by Daren Frease

Mr. Dusanek, Our Principal

Mickey Mouse on your ties
Really nice

Dog lover
Ultimate
Super
Amazing
Nice
Excellent
Kind

by Keagan Drish

Mr. Dusanek, Our Principal

Mickey Mouse is cool like you
Really nice

Do you like ties?
Uses a lot of smiles.
Super great
A great principal
Nice
Excellent principal
Kind

by Alejandra Giron